CONVERSATION

a debut collection b, ⌐————

Edited by Caitlin Conlon

"Samantha Nimmo's debut 'Conversations With The Sun' is one of the best collections of modern poetry you'll find. Laden with lush imagery and gorgeous illustrations, Nimmo's writing is a love letter to womanhood, motherhood, healing, love and, most of all, the self. The poet's words call to the strength within us all, and hold up a mirror for us to see it. For us to believe in it. This book is for anyone who walked through fire and came out glowing. For anyone who needs a reminder of all the light that's shining still, in the world around them, but most importantly, inside themselves. 'Conversations with the Sun' is a healing and empowering read, and I cannot recommend it enough." – *Lauren Poole, author of 'The Language of Ghosts'*

"Conversations With The Sun' is a breathtaking collection about loss, survival and liberation, with vividly painted stormy seas and sunrises that feel just out of reach. The emotional journey of the writer, too, feels just out of reach – with the voyage from devastating loss and betrayal through to self contentment surely echoing in the heart of any survivor. But the collection goes beyond this: for me, it is overwhelmingly about having the bravery to see the sunlight in the world and beneath our own skin. And, perhaps more importantly, letting that sunlight pour in. I wholeheartedly recommend this collection to anyone seeking a lighthouse in their own storm or a safe pair of hands to hold them while they heal." – *Sam Payne, author of 'This Boy is a Rainbow' and 'This Boy is a Constellation'*

"Samantha Nimmo's debut collection, 'Conversations With The Sun', is an ethereal depiction of hope. It is full to the brim with vivid imagery, overwhelming emotions, and beauty. Nimmo both rips your heart out and sews it back up for you. It is a privilege to accompany Nimmo on her journey from heartache into healing — watching her reclaim her heart as her own, and then make room in it for new love, is an incredible experience. The power that exudes from every page of this book is unmatched. Nimmo's words are pure light; you will close this book with the sun shining from within you. This debut collection is honest, vulnerable, unbelievably beautiful, and so worth the read."
— *Maddie McGlinchey, author of 'You're Still in my Passenger Seat...and Other Ghost Stories'*

Dedicated to my grandparents,
I am so incredibly proud to be your granddaughter.

Gran,
Thank you for always being my sun. Thank you for shining
no matter how many clouds tried to block you out.

Grandpa,
Thank you for teaching me to never stop asking questions.
Thank you for my curiosity.

Contents

I have found a friend
In the tender sun
"Rise," she tells me
"Your day is not done."

The Storm

I see her in
The mirror
The silver blade of a knife
The faint reflection on the window
A ghost a ghoul a girl
With red rimmed eyes and open palms
Fingers shaking
From gripping promises that slipped
Through the cracks anyway.
Where did they go?
The things you whispered in the dark
I she held them so tightly
And still they disappeared.
I see her
In the glass in the puddles in the
Arms of a boy she thought she loved.
I see her -
Press my hand to her cheek
Whisper: it wasn't love.
Love doesn't hurt.
Whisper: it wasn't your fault

Scream: *it wasn't my fault*

Sometimes it is a black dog
Sometimes it is a storm cloud
Other times
It is a serpent
Curled around my neck
So tight I can barely breathe

- Shapeshifter

I try to speak
But my words won't move.
My teeth get in the way
Of my tongue and
Bite
Bite
Bite
Until I bleed.

I don't know how to say your name
Without tasting copper
Anymore.

Sometimes it feels like
All this sadness
Has hollowed me out.
Scraped out my heart
Like gutting pumpkins on Halloween
Until I am so light I float
Up up up
A balloon without a string.
Sometimes it feels like
All this sadness
Has weighed me down.
My feet carry me in circles.
Always in circles.
Until I am so heavy I fall
Down down down
An anchor without a ship.

(when will I start feeling whole again?)

You held my head under the water
And then asked me why I was afraid to swim

It makes me feel dirty
Knowing your hands roamed my body
Ever pushed and pulled and pressed me
Into the shape you wanted

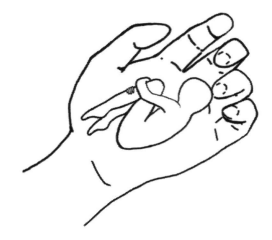

A Boy is Just a Boy Until

(after Sam Payne)

A boy is just a boy until he is a stargazer / calling you the
northern star / calling you at 3am to see if you're falling too
/ to see if he can catch you / and save you for a rainy day /
a boy is just a boy until he is the turning of the seasons / all
at once glacial and scorching / beautiful and bitter / a boy
is just a boy until he builds you a house / forgets to make it
a home / leaves the door open on his way out / a boy is
just a boy until he is a bruise / leaving you wondering when
he will finally fade / leaving you wondering when he
stopped being *just* a boy

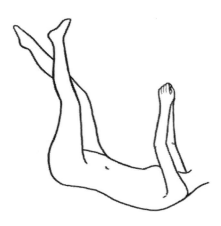

Do you remember the first time
You told me you loved me?
As if you were trying to find an excuse
For all the things you were about to do

Here's the thing
(that you never seemed to understand)
I was never yours.
I have never belonged to anybody but myself

You were just a thief in the night
(and in broad daylight)
Taking whatever you could get your hands on.

What happened to our promises?
Did they pack their bags and walk away
As easily as we did?
Or are they sitting in the ruins
Of our derelict love
Waiting for us to return?

-   Orphaned

He treated me like a masterpiece
Adorned in the finest frame
Behind bulletproof glass

But hidden in the attic.
Behind dusty boxes filled with the love of
Long forgotten lovers

Nobody could steal me
If they couldn't find me

-    prized possession

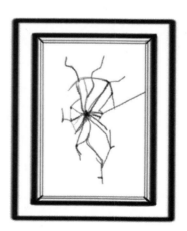

Like King Midas
Everything you touch
C h a n g e s
But instead of gold
It all dissolves to dust

-       I watched my heart

        f

            a

                l

                    l

    through the cracks between your fingers

You poured poison
Into your own cup
And then screamed
"Look at what you've done to me"

We were all
Peach pits and cherry stalks
Bruised flesh discarded
All stem and no bloom
Heads bitten off of roses
Petals spat out with curses
Crushed under ungrateful teeth
Bitten tongues and chewed lips
Swollen with excuses

I reached for you in the darkness

But you pretended not to see

And as you walked away I howled

WHY AM
I SO
EASY TO
LEAVE

In an alternate universe
Where we never broke up
I am cracked wide open
Cavernous, and echoing
With distant promises.

In an alternate universe
Where we're still in love
I never find magic in my veins
Still timid, unwaveringly obedient
The word 'no' is forever perched
On the tip of my tongue
Always too scared to jump

- In an alternate universe, I wish for this one

Co-Star Says I Should Be Honing the Skill of Being Able to Ask for Help:

(after Lauren Poole)

And I want to laugh.
I've never been good at admitting when I need help staying
afloat / in fact, I think I would use my last breath to say
"I'm fine" / even as the water caresses my lungs

But I know co-star is right

I know there should not be any shame slipping off my lips
when I ask for a life raft / I understand that eventually I
will get tired of treading water / and have to reach for aid
(It's happened before / but I keep wading back into the
open ocean anyway)

When all my yesterdays taste of sea salt / how do I beg my
tomorrows to taste like lavender and peaches and honey /
(God, what I'd give to feel like I deserve some sweetness) /
I've been haunted all my life by the fear of looking weak /
and I have yet to drown the ghosts / (they swim they swim
they swim)

Co-star says I should be honing the skill of being able to
ask for help and I say I know I know I know

Maybe this time I will

You said you needed space
So I made a whole universe.
The planets revolved around your smile.
I forced myself to be stronger than gravity. I forced myself
to let you go.

You said you needed space
So I made a whole universe.
Made myself a star (only existing as a product of breaking
apart). A pinprick of light in the
aching darkness.

You said you needed space
So I made a whole universe.
Still, you told me to dim the light.
Didn't I tell you I wanted some time alone? You say.
I gave you galaxies to be alone in. I say.

Then why are you still here? You ask.

And I realise I don't have an answer

Why haven't I left yet?

You reached past my ribs and grabbed my heart
While it was still beating
And through the pain all I could think was:
At least you were holding me
One last time

I am afraid
That if I speak
My heart will stumble out of my mouth
Onto my lap
And everyone will see
Just how fractured it really is

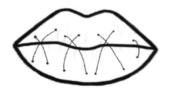

I hand-stitched
Each star into the sky
So you would have light to see
Through the blanket of darkness
That we huddled beneath
But all you did was shield your eyes
And look away,
Complaining that it was too bright
To love me under

Sentences cemented themselves
To my throat
Paragraphs polluted my lungs
Consonants collected in
The valves of my heart

- Even my words turned against me

I sliced open
My still beating heart
To show you its core
And you just brushed off the blood
And asked me to
Not be so messy next time

The ghost of you still s e e p s through

walls to reach me.

Haven't you taken enough?

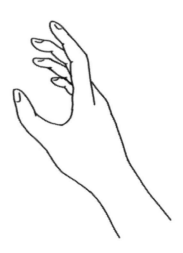

I've been thinking about us
How our ending was purple;
Red lipstick stains and
Blue regrets
Merging every time our lips met.

A fresh bruise

We were a balancing act / a held breath / a slow dance on the precipice of a cliff / how many times will I walk off the edge? / how many times will I jump just to see if I can fly? / how long will it take me to admit that / falling is better / than the feeling that we're going nowhere?

You had a fuse as short
As the burnt candle wick
Of our romance –
By the end there was only wax pooled on the floor
Warning of the explosion to come

- Where do moths go when all the light is gone?

Sometimes I let myself think about
Who I was before you -
But only for a second.
Only long enough to remember
Mascara clumped together
But not yet running
The thrill of putting on stop-light-red lipstick
And having it stay unsmudged
Strawberry stained fingers
Pale pink not crimson.
Sometimes I let myself think about
Who I could've been if I hadn't met you
But only for a second.
It is a fantasy too sweet to bear

The stars are sick of hearing about you.
They tell me to quit chasing heartbreak
As though it's the adventure of a lifetime
I ask them how? *How?*
Because if heartbreak isn't a journey then I'm going nowhere and
I ask them why? *Why* must I give it up?
At least I know what's going to happen with you.
I've always hated surprises and it hurts
less and less each time I run down this road and
I ask them when? *When* will I stop myself from crashing into a dead-end
Making the same mistakes and expecting different results and
I ask them if they've spoken to you.

Do you tell the stars about me, too?

The Shelter

i have run out of
excuses for you

and i have run out
of excuses not to
love myself

I will not kneel
In front of a king
Again
I refuse to be
A loyal servant
To a man who wears a crown
Of stolen gold

Dashboard Confessional

things I'd tell you if you'd only ask // things I'd ask you if you'd only tell me

(after Lauren Poole)

I know how to swim / but sometimes I don't want to / sometimes floating feels so heavy / sometimes the weight of happiness feels like stones in my pockets / sometimes I yearn to sink to the sand

I am strong / I know I am strong but / sometimes it feels that strength is taken for granted / just because I am strong does not mean I don't feel the weight of everything I carry / it doesn't mean my back isn't breaking / it just means I keep dutifully walking forward / despite it all

I want us to be evergreen / *I* want to be evergreen / I want to let the hills swallow me whole / I want to live in mother nature's throat / but I can't stop writing about the fucking ocean / and isn't that really the problem? / I want the things that don't want me / I want the things that scare the sense out of me / I don't know how to live between the lines / when everything looks so much brighter on the other side of them

Are you happy? / really happy? / truly happy? / I know the sea is calling you home / I think you were born in the wrong skin / I swear you were supposed to be a siren / and what I wouldn't give to be a victim of your voice / would you be happy then? / we'd both get our wish / you could live beneath the waves and I / I wouldn't even need the stones

How does it feel to live between Gaia's fingers? / is her palm as gentle as it looks? / her heart line seems so deep / do you lose yourself in it like I wish I could? / are her eyes the same green as mine? / (say yes say yes say yes) / will you ask her if she's lost a daughter?

Will you tell her to come find me?

You curse the rain
As if the flowers
You fawn over
Don't bathe in its presence

You were always like that -
Wanting beauty
While refusing to weather the storms

I used to look for you
In the morning sun
Sneaking through the gap between my curtains
In the candy floss pink
Of sunsets that set the sky alight.
With hope and love and
With my eyes to the sky

Now I look for you
In the creaky floorboards
That I always step on in the middle of the night
In the shadows
Creeping up behind me with their claws out.
With fear and dread and
My eyes to the ground.

-    When will I stop looking?

It's been 1 2 3 4 5 years / and I'm still trying to catch my
breath / it seems my lungs are still reeling / from the sting
of my begging / it takes everything / *everything* / I have /
not to write you as the villain / in a teenage fairytale / but I
can't even stand / to spell your name /besides / you taught
me / 1 2 3 4 5 years ago / that there is no red riding hood /
or valiant knight

only wolves

Does the mention of my name
Make your lip curl?
Do I leave crescent moons
On the palms of your hands?
Do they remind you of the night we spent
Underneath the stars?
Do the poems I wrote you
Come alive in your daydreams?
Do they sound like a happy ending?
What I'm trying to say is –
Do I still drive you as mad as I used to?

I am so much more
Than the way my name sounded
In your mouth
(Like breathless prayer
A request for redemption)
Than the way my eyes looked
Reflected in yours
(Like a forest fighting
Against rising tides)
Or the way my skin felt
Under your clumsy hands
(Like clay just before it cracks –
As though the weight of us was too much to bear)

In Some Other Universe Where We've Yet to Fall Apart

You kiss me like I don't taste of regret / I adore you like it doesn't hurt / You tell me we can get a dog / and I believe you / (I believe you'd face your fears for me) / (but you prove me wrong) / the shower always runs a little too hot / but the burning soothes me / *it feels better than you do*

We make promises we won't keep / and I make wishes that won't come true / (like for you to dig out the parts of me you keep underneath your fingernails / and piece me back together)

We spend years running in circles / until my feet don't know any other route / I keep saying that I love you / until the words have lost all meaning / *but it's a nice routine* / and you smile back every time

I write you letters but you say you can't read my handwriting / we both know you're lying / I sleep walk through every day because I am so tired / of carrying your mistakes around / my back hurts / but you never offer to lighten the load / and there is a mutual understanding that it was all my fault anyway

And we end. / Eventually.

How many years does it take, I wonder? / does it leave me aching when I realise that what we had was never love? / not because I'm mourning us / but because I'm so relieved / *that there is something better out there*

Lies I Like To Tell Myself

1. Your name doesn't echo through the places in me you hollowed out anymore –

2. I filled them with love – stuffed to the brim with whatever parts I could salvage from our wreck. (As if that means they are any less empty.)

3. My skin has forgotten your fingerprints – my thighs a memory foam mattress finally smoothed out

4. This is the last poem I'll write about you (just like the last) (just like the one before that)

I was a sunflower
Bright, beautiful and brave
But all you wanted was a rose
Sweet, sensible and safe

There is nothing
Left to say.
You didn't listen
Even when there was.
I hope you know
I'm not sorry
For what I told you
Only that I didn't share it sooner.
My only regret is
That I loved you more
Than I loved myself

How lovely it is to realise
That there are whole weeks
That go by when I do not remember
The sound of your voice
Or the scent of your shampoo
Or feel the lingering warmth of your body
Pressed into the sheets on your side of the bed

– one day i'll forget
you altogether

I look in the mirror
And no longer see your hands

-    Recovery

I OWE YOU NOTHING

i owe myself everything

I will not beg you to love me
Instead I will beg my body for forgiveness
For not standing up for her sooner

A Small List of Gratitudes

1. the sky is purple tonight. for once I am not scared of its expanse. for once I want to dive right in without fear of losing myself in it. (for once *I want to lose myself in it*)

2. the violets won't stop blooming. they've been flowering since June but summer has not worn them down. (like it has me)

3. the plums are still fresh even though I forgot I bought them. they fight the rot long enough to stain my tongue ~~the colour of your favourite wine~~. they fight the rot and that is all that matters. (I will not let myself find you in their flesh)

4. the memory foam on your side of the bed has forgotten. it is smooth now and soft. I got the stains out, too. the ones from when you ~~spilled Sangria~~ no ~~dropped your toast face down and let the jam spread~~ no ~~let the raspberry juice drip down your chin and seep into the sheets~~ no. the ones that dried like rose petal bruises. (you know the ones I mean)

5. the lilac hair dye I wanted came back into stock today. maybe I'll finally buy it. (it's about time I did something just for me)

You call me
Pretty
You forget I am
Powerful
You call me
Beautiful
You forget I am
Brave
You call me
Sexy
You forget I am
Smart
You call me

And I don't answer

I wear oversized jumpers
Think oversized thoughts
Feel oversized love

- I don't know how to do things by halves

Things That Keep Me Up At Night

I wonder how many universes I have died in / how many universes I've wanted to die in / it's 2:05am / I should fall asleep / (stop watching the clock) / I can feel the minutes slipping through my fingers / tumbling off my thumb nail / sliding down my palm to their death / like I'm some sort of grave / a tomb for time / how much do I have left? / do autumn leaves fear the fall? / if the sun exploded it would take us eight minutes to know / would I even want to know? / I think that's a good way to go / if I have to go let the sun swallow me whole / let me leave in her embrace / let me be all light and molten gold / the silver moon would weep in second place / is that thunder or just a car going past? / is the car going to go through the front door of the flat downstairs again? / why am I so scared of thunder, anyway? / I once read that we dislike people who possess the traits we hate in ourselves / maybe that's why / maybe I'm jealous of the lightning / how many times has my name stained someone's cheeks and tongue and fingertips? / I want to know what they say about me / I don't want to know what they say about me / is my baby breathing? / is my partner breathing? / am I breathing? / look, I know the last words I said to my gran were I'll see you soon but / I'm going to have to keep her waiting / I'm not ready to go just yet / hey, look at that - / I'm not ready to go just yet / I'M NOT READY TO GO JUST YET / it's 2:07am / *where's the off switch?*

I have sewn stars
Into my heart
As a reminder to myself
To embrace the light

It is not my fault
That you never learned
To appreciate the beauty of the wild
You were far too civilised
To understand
Why I wanted to run with wolves

You see me as a
peach pit picked clean by brittle teeth.
Exposed.
You expect me to unravel or soften but I am all cruel
concrete -
Even as juice drips from the pads of your fingers
and you lick them clean
Golden strands of me haunt your fever dreams
tangled in your hairbrush and wrapped around your ring
finger
like some sort of morbid promise.
You want me to be some tangible, tricky thing
to hold between your thumb and forefinger but
I am only human.
And that means you cannot contain me in metaphors.

I will always be too much for you to hold.

When they are mere seeds
Bedded in soil
Do flowers know
That one day
They will reach the light
They so desperately long for?
Or,
Like the rest of us,
Do they just keep pushing forward
Hoping for the best
Hoping that it won't all be for nothing

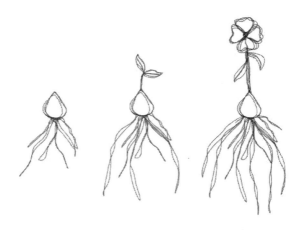

Love me like you love the spring flowers
Gently, sweetly, in awe
Of their beauty,
Looking to them for signs of change
Of better things to come

I still ask after you in the mirror, you know / search for you in shop window reflections / I shouldn't tell you this / but I still haven't worn that dress - / I guess I haven't let you go after all

I'm just writing to say that / I won't leave the door unlocked anymore / I want the spare key back. / I find you in burnt toast and bitter coffee / sponge cake and hot chocolate with cream / and I am sick, so sick, of the taste you leave

I know I should have done this years ago but / you were holding on to me so tight I was scared / I would crumble without it / but I haven't. / And I won't. / In fact, I feel stronger than ever.

I think I'll wear that dress tomorrow.

- Dear Insecurities

My heart is
Like a prisoner pounding at the bars
Like a sunflower seed desperate to reach the light
Like lightning striking the same spot twice
Like wine drunk girls stumbling down stairs –
Like the safety net ready to catch them
Like an atheist knelt in prayer
(faithless, full of contradictions)

You can take me as I am
Or not at all
I don't need to be stitched back together
I have never been anything less than whole

Can I tell you a secret?

I can't sleep. Everything is cold without you. I wish you were here. (Sorry, that was three.)

What I mean is you are like the sun. A star. I guess it's the same thing, except I see you every

hour of the day every minute of the night it's as though nothing can dim your light. Nothing can outshine you. Look, I'm rambling, but all I know is that you are sunshine and warmth and toasted marshmallows in the middle of summer.

(I don't want to go back to living in the dark.)

Reasons I Cry

(after Mary Lambert)

I cry because my son is still so small yet so much bigger
than he was when he was born / I cry because he claps
when I dance and I don't want the world to steal that joy
that softness that light / I cry because I don't know how to
stop the thieves

I cry because there are still flowers even though the world
seems so cold / I cry because I am still so young but I feel
so old

I cry because the sun won't return my love letters / I cry
because hope is a living thing but I think I am killing it /
like that aloe vera plant I overwatered / I cry because I
don't know how to stop giving

I cry because I am an ocean / that I cannot find the bottom
of / and it terrifies me that I do not know what lurks in the
depths

I cry because I am finally forgiving myself for loving a boy
with broken glass for hands

I cry for the past I can't change even though it cleaves me
open / and for the wounds I can't hold closed / I cry
because I don't want to bleed on my future

I cry because I have somehow convinced somebody to love
me / so much that he has opened his chest to hand me his
heart / and I cry because I don't want to leave a scar

I cry because I have taken things I shouldn't have / to replace what was taken from me and / I cry because all I can do about it is write poetry

I cry because I know that it is not enough

Is this what better looks like?
Brushed hair and clean clothes
Another load in the washing machine

Is this what better tastes like?
The second cup of coffee
Cherry kisses
And not a hint of bitter regret

Is this what better sounds like?
Sleep coated whispers
Soft and quiet
(I am not afraid of the silence anymore)

Is this what better feels like?
Moths caught in my throat
Beating their wings to get free

Never quite as welcome as butterflies

I always yearned for happiness
As if it were simple.
As if I could just wake up one day
To a bright yellow world –
As though sunshine had leaked into everything.
As though by painting a smile
Onto the canvas of my lips
I could scare sadness away.

Instead, I looked for it wherever I could.
Poking through concrete
Peeking through blinds
Pressed into the palm of my hand.

I found it everywhere.

I am a snowdrop
Not even the hardest frost
Can stop my growth –
Reaching for
Even the slightest ray of sun

-   I will bloom even when nothing else can

I want you to see
The roadmap of my body
Follow it until you get lost
I want you to see
The pieces I glued back together
With shaky hands
The edges that will never smooth out
I want you to see
The tiger stripes climbing my hips
Evidence of growth and strength –
Skin not quite as smooth as it once was

I don't want you to fix me
I want you to love me anyway

If I Did What I Was Told

I would be a bright red rose
Cut at the root and stuck in stale water.
I would be skin stretched over bone
Losing all the softness I have learned to treasure.
I would be all teeth and no tongue
A silent, stunning, sad smile.
I would be the ghost of a heart that died too young
Haunting and hunting and volatile.
If I did what I was told
I might've been happy for a while
But all these mistakes I've made
Are making living worthwhile.

Loss sounds like
The silent seconds in the wake of a shattered glass
The clinking of teeth against long cold cups of coffee
(black, no sugar)
The wind racing past your ears blowing knotted hair off of
tear-stained cheeks
It sounds like hitched inhales and held breaths
It sneaks into all the empty seconds cupped in the palm of
my hand
Lukewarm and mild.

No matter how loud I live,
I cannot drown it out.

I want to fill books
With the things my heart says –
No – screams
Into sunsets
And starry nights
And I want to give them to
All the little girls who think
That nobody knows how they feel

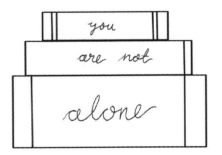

Do you think
The stars know
We watch the night undress them
And lay their beauty bare
Do you think
They are aware
Of their audience down here
Do you think
They get self-conscious
In the light of the moon
Do you think
If I tried hard enough
I could be a star, too?

In The Event of Emergency

(after Sarah Kay)

I would have so much more to give if I had enough
Time. I want to stuff it in to my pockets
Grab fistfuls and tuck them safely away.
Give this time to my son
Tell him I only wish I had been there
To spend it with him.
Give the words on the tip of my tongue to my father
He is the one who taught me how to use them
I know he will use them well.
Give my mother all my dreams
For she knows I will meet her in them.
To my grandmother, give my
Stubbornness and fire for
I stole my first spark from her years ago.
Return my curiosity to my grandfather
He will search for the answers in encyclopaedias
and dictionaries in all the languages he knows.
Maybe he will find them where I could not.
Give my hair and lungs and smile lines
To the beaches and jungles and deserts
That I longed to visit. Return them to the wild.
My poems and stories and handwritten notes
belong to my heart
Please give them back to it.
You'll find it in his chest. (It has been his for years)
Give the pads of my feet to the street I grew up in
and my skinned knees to the tree in the front garden.
Give my scars to the stars and my eyes to the sun

(I always wanted to look directly at it)
Leave whatever music is still in my veins
To my brother. He can keep it alive.
To my friends, give my laughter and liver
So I can toast a final glass of wine. (Rosé
in the biggest glass they can find)
Finally, give my gritted teeth and clenched fists
To the little girls just learning to fight.
Tell them to never stop.
Tell them I will always fight with them.

The Sun
Seeker

Love sounds like
Your sleep-coated voice at 3am
Looks like
The way you stare at me
As though you've discovered the secrets of the universe
Smells like
Coffee in the morning and breakfast in bed
Feels like
Your lips on my forehead and fingers laced through my hair
Tastes like
Honey
Enveloping my throat until
All I can say is
Your name

I want
To spend
The rest of my life
Looking at the stars
With you
To memorise how
Your eyes dance as
You track constellations
To plan a life
On the moon with you
And know that I would never
Miss the sun's embrace
As long as you were there
To hold me, instead

How lovely it is
Waking up to
Those ocean grey eyes
- I'm not afraid to swim anymore

Love sneaks in through the window
Way past curfew
Settles down under the duvet
Helps herself to a cup of coffee in the morning.
Finds the spare key no matter where you hide it.
Comes back no matter how many
Times you tell her it's over.
She pries open the bars around your heart
And curls up in the warmth –
Makes her home in the parts of you
That you thought would never thaw

(She reminds you that you have always been
Enough for her)

If You Are What You Love I Am

(after Skyler Saunders)

If you are what you love I am coffee with frothed milk and
hazelnut syrup / bold brush strokes / classic novels and
handwritten poems / I am lilac nail polish and pale pink
promises / I am the rain on the roof of the car / the
rhythm and release / the exhale after years of held breaths
/ I am sunflowers and potted plants and dandelions
peaking through the cracks in search of the sun / I am the
sun they seek / if you are what you love, I am love / I am
love

I Live Because

There's still coffee left to drink / and cake left to eat / and cups of tea to burn my tongue on

Because I haven't even read all the books on the shelf never mind the ones waiting in my basket / and I've not been annoyed by all the songs my son's toys sing yet / God, my son / if there was ever a reason to live, it is him

I live because the walls still have more room for my grandmother's paintings / because I want to hear all my grandfather's stories / and marvel at how he never runs out of them / because my dad's eyes are hard but they soften when he looks at us / and I haven't studied them long enough yet / because my mother's heartbeat tells me "you can you can you can" / and I want to see how much taller than me my brother will get / (how much he will grow)

I live because I have not yet explored every chamber of my partner's heart / and because Sidney's sonnets remind me that *I am a fool* / to look anywhere but my own heart / to ease the aching

Because I have so many mistakes left to make

I live for the me that didn't want to / for the little girl full to the brim with questions that I haven't found the answer to yet -

I live because I will always have more questions to ask /
and I am learning that

the questions are more important than the answers anyway

How I Know You Haven't Gone Anywhere

Because the world is still spinning. Because when I knocked over a flower pot today it cracked in the shape of an 'A'. Because my baby smiles and laughs at the picture of a parrot you painted that's hanging in my living room. Because if you were really gone, you'd have taken all the colours with you but the world is not in grey-scale. Because you are infinite. Because you never could be contained by any one thing. Because you are in everything beautiful now. Everything beautiful is you.

The wild
Is calling for me
Tugging at the strings of my heart
With promises of adventure

How can I say no?

What will they say of me
When I am gone?
Please let it be
"What a dreamer she was
How fiercely she loved
How fearlessly she fell."

This body is made
From cherry tree blossoms
From bitter winter rain
From scorching summer sun
It's a force of nature
That you'd be lucky to see
And luckier to love

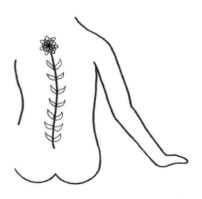

I was scared
That my heart wouldn't have enough room left
To love you the way you deserve to be loved

But instead, love has made a home
Within my bones
And shines through my pores.

So darling, if you're looking for love
Look for the light

There is something delicate
And fragile and
Oh so
Beautiful
About times like these.
It's in the air –
In the palm of your hand –
On the tip of your tongue.
Can't you taste it?
Sweet like honey and just as
Golden.

-    Hope

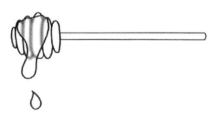

Love
Rolls off my tongue
Every day every hour every minute
It is soft and sweet and I wonder
If you can ever have too much of a good thing

I am spring storms
(you are scared of thunder)
I am an ocean
(you say the waves are too fierce)
I am wild roses
(you try to trim my thorns)
I am untamed, *untameable*
I am all heart –
Entirely too much and somehow never enough
For you.

I am a lot of things -
But sorry isn't one of them.

You do not have to love me
I will not fade away to dust
Without your touch

I have enough love already inside me
To fill a whole sky with stars

I wish I had
A hundred lifetimes
To show you all the beautiful gifts
This world has to offer.

To show you that *you are* the most beautiful gift
This world has ever offered

I want to write great plays about you
Novels filled with pretty words
Pages filled with poems.
But you cannot be contained by syllables
And similes. Metaphors and musings
Are no match for a being made of pure light,
Sweet boy,
I'm afraid all I have is this heart
Where you will always have a home

Gentle,
My love,
That's what you are.
Soft,
Tender,
Everything you do
Is a whisper.
As though you are
Slow dancing with life
A careful waltz

- It's beautiful to watch

They said we were made
Of sugar and spice
And everything nice –
Pretty, delicate, little things.
They failed to say
We are powerful and brave
Made of snowdrops and steel
We have fire running through our veins

Advice From the Sun
for Lauren

One day rising won't feel like a chore and your sky will be
swathed in all the colours of forgiveness. The clouds will
dance with you and let you lead. They will follow your steps
and never once stand on your toes. They have been
practicing for you.

One day setting won't feel like a cold kiss on your forehead.
One day the darkness will be nothing but soft, a warm
blanket wrapped around your shoulders and your shoulders
will be so light so light so light. The night is sorry. She does
not mean to be so consuming but she cannot help loving
your heart. She promises to be less selfish. She says she will
let me love you, too.

One day the ghosts will settle like dust on the window ledge
sparkling in the morning dew. One day you will rise with
me and we will not stop rising we will not stop rising dear
god we will not stop rising one day

you will rise higher than I do

i have no plan
only love
only hope

Acknowledgements

To Mum:
I cannot possibly thank you enough. For everything you do for me. For being an incredible mum, and friend. For supporting me and loving me unconditionally. For being an amazing artist and passing along that love to me. For everything and so much more. I love you to the university and back.

To Dad:
I don't know where to begin but look – I wrote a book! Thank you for my love of writing, for passing along the inability to escape the words. It is both a blessing and a curse but I am eternally grateful for it. Even between the two of us, I'm still not sure we could ever find a word to sum up how lucky I feel to be your daughter. "Thank you" just isn't enough.

To my friends and family:
I am so incredibly grateful for your love and support. Thank you thank you thank you for everything you do for me.

To Wren:
I don't know if you'll ever read this, but if you do, thank you for being pure light. I love you more than you will ever know. (And I'm sorry for writing embarrassing poetry about you!)

To Zac:
For being the best partner I could ever imagine. A million thank yous for always cheering me on and being by my side through everything. For giving me so much love to write about.

To the poetry community:
There are too many of you to name. You know who you are. Thank you for every single like, comment and message. Without you, this book likely wouldn't exist.

To Lauren, Sam and Maddie:
Thank you so much for your incredible advanced reviews. You have no idea how much they warmed my heart (and made me tear up!) Mostly, thank you for being my (incredibly talented) friends.

To Caitlin Conlon:
Thank you for being an amazing editor and for all your support!

To everyone reading this:
Thank you thank you thank you thank you thank you. I cannot believe you are holding this book in your hands, it still feels like a dream. Your support means the world to me.

About the Author

Samantha Nimmo is a twenty year old poet and illustrator from Scotland. She is currently studying English at university and juggles essay writing and poetry with being a mum to a perfect little boy. When she is not writing, she enjoys eating pizza, drinking rosé, buying (even more) house plants and reading any book she can get her hands on.

This is her first poetry collection.

You can find more of her work on Instagram @sn.poetry

Printed in Great Britain
by Amazon